The Unknown God

The Unknown God

Searching for Spiritual Fulfilment

Alister McGrath

William B. Eerdmans Publishing Company
Grand Rapids, Michigan

First published by
Lion Publishing plc
Sandy Lane West, Oxford, England

This edition published 1999 in the United States of America by
Wm. B. Eerdmans Publishing Co.
255 Jefferson Ave. S.E., Grand Rapids, Michigan 49503

Printed and bound in Spain

03 02 01 00 99 5 4 3 2 1

ISBN 0-8028-3864-2

Contents

1 A Spiritual Hunger 7

2 Searching for the Land of Dreams 12

3 The Great Projection Theory 18

4 Plato's Cave 26

5 Beauty beyond Description 34

6 The Pearl of Great Price 42

7 The Rich Fool 49

8 The Lost Sheep 54

9 A Royal Invitation 59

10 The Unknown God 65

11 The Precious Gift 72

12 The Secret of the Kingdom 76

13 The Ransom 83

14 The Divine Healer 90

15 The Dawn of New Life 100

16 Living in Hope 108

17 The End of All Our Longing 116

A Spiritual Hunger

1

A noted philosopher once commented that when people had plenty to eat they turned their minds to thinking great thoughts. The point he was making is simple. You need to make sure of your physical survival before you can do some serious thinking. Yet one of the most curious things about serious human thought is that it often focuses on the theme of emptiness. Having satisfied their physical hunger, people become aware of a deeper kind of hunger – a longing for something that will really satisfy.

So what is it that really satisfies us? For some, the answer will lie in achievements – doing something that makes a difference to the world, and leaves us feeling that we have made our mark on things. For others, the answer will lie in personal relationships: the only things that are genuinely fulfilling are the relationships established with significant others. Yet, however we choose to define ideas such as 'fulfilment' or 'satisfaction', it is a simple fact of life that these are widely regarded as the things that make life worthwhile.

Many people feel that any kind of fulfilment or satisfaction has eluded them. 'Whatever it is that has the power to satisfy truly and deeply, I have yet to find it.' For some, it is something that is for ever beyond human grasp. Some of the things that seem to assure fulfilment fail to live up to their promises. Plato, perhaps the greatest of the classical Greek philosophers, commented that human nature was like a leaky jar. No sooner have you filled it than it begins to empty. If there is something that has the power to fulfil truly and deeply, then for many it is something unknown, hidden in mystery and secrecy. We move from one thing and place to another, lingering only long enough to discover that it is not what we were hoping for before renewing our quest for fulfilment. The great certainty of our time seems to be that satisfaction is nowhere to be found. We roam around, searching without finding, yearning without being satisfied.

So often our anticipation of what we will find proves vastly preferable to what we actually find.

The pursuit of happiness is often said to be one of the most fundamental human rights. Yet this happiness proves astonishingly elusive. So often, those who actively pursue happiness find that it slips through their

THE ANTIQUE DEALER
Heinrich Ede (1819–85)

fingers. It is an ideal which is easily put into words, yet seems to remain beyond our reach. We have long become used to the fact that the richest people in this world are often the most miserable, yet fail to see the irony of this.

Perhaps this is just one of the sad paradoxes of being human. Maybe we will have to get used to the fact that we are always going to fail in our search for happiness. Part of the cruel irony of human existence seems to be that the things we thought would make us happy fail to do so. 'To travel hopefully is a better thing than to arrive' (Robert Louis Stevenson). Why? Because so often our anticipation of what we will find proves vastly preferable to what we actually find on our arrival. If that's the way things are, then we had better get used to them. There would seem to be little

> The mind of a man is miserable and longs for happiness. It can only hope for this because change is possible, otherwise the mind could neither move from happiness to misery, nor from misery to happiness. Under the rule of an all-powerful and good God nothing but the mind's sin and his justice could have made it miserable. And nothing but the mind's goodness and the Lord's rewarding of it can make it happy. Yet even the goodness is a gift from the one whose reward is the happiness.
> AUGUSTINE OF HIPPO, *CONFESSIONS*

point in continually hoping for something better, when we have been so often disappointed in the past.

Maybe. Or there might be another way of looking at this basic human experience. Maybe it is trying to tell us something. Maybe it is pointing to something – something which we do not yet know, but which is somehow hinted at by what we do know. It seems as if there *is* something that lies beyond us that exercises a hidden attraction upon us. Perhaps a new world lies beyond the horizon of our experience, a world that we only know through hints and rumours. It is like living by the ocean shore, and occasionally seeing strange plants washed up on the sand – a signal that there is something beyond our horizon that we have yet to discover.

Suppose our longing for fulfilment points to something we have yet to discover? What if our yearning is a clue to the meaning of the universe?

Through Art we are sometimes sent – indistinctly, briefly – revelations not to be achieved by rational thought.

It is like that small mirror in the fairy tales – you glance in it and what you see is not yourself; for an instant you glimpse the Inaccessible, where no horse or magic carpet can take you. And the soul cries out for it...

ALEXANDER SOLZHENITSYN,
ONE WORD OF TRUTH

Suppose our longing for fulfilment points to something we have yet to discover – something that really has the ability to satisfy us? What if our yearning is a clue to the meaning of the universe? What if our sense of emptiness is like a signpost, pointing us in a certain direction? What if we were to explore what that direction might be, and what might await us?

This book is an exploration of the theme of human longing, and what it points to. To begin with, we will explore the theme of longing in a little more detail.

2 Searching for the Land of Dreams

Deep down, many of us long for something that is really worthwhile. We are looking for something that really matters. There seems to be something about human nature that makes it want to long for something life-changing. While many people are troubled by the thought of dying, others are disturbed by a much more profound anxiety – that we might die without having really begun to live.

The great Roman politician Marcus Tullius Cicero once wrote that he wished we could all die when we were young. Why? Because then we would not live to see our hopes and ideals destroyed by the harsh realities of life. So often our dreams come unravelled. We were told that the First World War would be 'the war to end all wars'. Sadly, it just didn't work out like that. The words were powerful – but empty. If we can put a man on the moon, we were told, we can do just about anything. Yet poverty, disease and war remain great problems.

Many young people dream of a world in which education and proper distribution of wealth would eliminate poverty, disease and war. One of the reasons Marxism appealed to so many young people in the 1960s was its vision of a future society free from all the ills and pain of the present. That vision offered hope for the future. It also offered a real place in history to those who would bring about the revolution which would usher in this new period in history. Yet the dream fell apart, as it became increasingly clear that it was founded on illusions and distortions.

The popular songs of periods of protest often echo such great hopes, speaking of an end to human misery. Yet many of those who wrote such songs look back on them later from the perspective of a greater experience of life, and wonder how they managed to be so naïve when they were younger. The second half of their lives is spent trying to forget, deny or explain away the first half. 'We were young then, and it all seemed real and within our grasp. Now, it just seems hopelessly idealistic and unrealistic.' Hints of cynicism often abound. 'I was naïve then. Now I've grown out of that kind of thing.'

While many people are troubled by the thought of dying, others are disturbed by a much more profound anxiety – that we might die without having really begun to live.

Yet the hope *was* real. The longing to do something

worthwhile *was* real. They seemed to have attached themselves to something which, in the end, could not support them fully. It is not the hope or longing which are at fault, but the goals to which we allow them to become attached. Experience seems to teach us that every time we long for something, we are disappointed by its outcome. It is very easy to allow this to develop into cynicism. 'There is no point in longing, caring or hoping – you just get hurt and disappointed by what happens.'

'I wish that someone had told me that when you get to the top, there's nothing there.'

It is easy to see this sense of hopelessness in other areas of life. Many of us know of ambitious people who have made it their goal to get to the top. This often involves immense sacrifices on their part – such as long hours at work, with little time for friends and family. Finally, usually late in life, they achieve their goal. Initially, there is an enormous sense of elation and satisfaction. 'I've done it!' Yet somehow this seems to give way to a somewhat different experience. 'Was it worth it?' One leading author was once asked the following question: 'What would you have liked to have been told at the age of sixteen, which you now know to be true?' His answer? 'I wish that someone had told me that when you get to the top, there's nothing there.' Again, we have that feeling of emptiness, made more poignant by the fact that we had hoped that we would achieve something that would finally satisfy.

Often, it seems as if we are pioneers in search of a promised land flowing with milk and honey. The hope of arrival keeps us going. We cross a mountain range, hoping that we will see the promised land ahead, stretching into the distance, and inviting us to enter in and possess it. Instead we find ourselves climbing that mountain range,

PARADISE
From a book on the Seven Wonders of the World

only to discover that another lies beyond it. We have still further to go before we discover the promised land. Paradise seems to have been postponed yet again.

This theme of longing for something magical, satisfying and fulfilling is found in literature down the ages. The biblical theme of the Garden of Eden is often seen as an image of a tranquil paradise in which human longings are satisfied. It can be seen developed in the image of a tropical island, against whose luscious golden shores the warm blue ocean laps, where the air is clear and unpolluted, and where all human troubles can be forgotten. It is a profoundly attractive vision. Yet, for most of us, it is nothing more than a dream, easily dismissed as a consolation of our own making to help us get through the grey and grim grittiness of our existence.

And yet we are still left with that nagging question. Can we really dismiss this human longing for something which seems to lie beyond us as a delusion, however pleasant, which merely distracts us from the harsher truths of real life? Or might this sense of longing be a signpost, pointing us to that promised land?

> It must be so – Plato, thou reason'st well! –
> Else whence this pleasing hope, this fond desire,
> This longing after immortality?
> Or whence this secret dread, and inward horror,
> Of falling into naught? Why shrinks the soul
> Back on herself, and startles at destruction?
> 'Tis the divinity that stirs within us;
> 'Tis heaven itself that points out an hereafter,
> And intimates eternity to man.
> JOSEPH ADDISON, *CATO*, V.I.i

3 The Great Projection Theory

Our deep sense that there has to be more to things might well be a signpost to something greater. It might lead us to a door which, once thrown open, leads to fulfilment. Or it might be a tantalizing glimpse of something which never was and never will be. It might be like a young boy who longed for a bicycle for his eleventh birthday, and was given

instead the complete philosophical works of Kierkegaard in the original Danish. That night, he dreamt of owning and riding the most wonderful bicycle in the world. It was a dream, and even in that dream he knew it was only a dream – but it was still a dream which brought him a fulfilment and joy which Kierkegaard did not.

There will always be a suspicion that we project our longings and desires, and give them a reality which they do not and should not possess. Some would argue that a longing for immortality leads us to invent the idea of eternal life, just as a longing for meaning causes us to dream up the idea of God. These are to be seen as an attempt to console ourselves, a drug which we have created to ease our pain.

They are something that we long for – and is not the fact that we long for them enough to allow us to explain them away? This is the Great Projection Theory, which declares that we have fallen into the habit of projecting our hopes and longings onto some imaginary supernatural screen, and believing that the result is as real as the world of sense and experience.

It is true that the longing for something does not make it true or real. It is easy for us to imagine the situation of someone who has become lost in the great deserts of New Mexico or the Sahara. As she painfully and slowly tries to find her way to civilization, she becomes increasingly aware of her thirst. She longs for water. As she makes her way over the barren surface, she desperately looks around for water to cool her cracked lips and give her new strength. Perhaps she will find an oasis, or a spring of crystal clear water bursting forth from the living rocks of the desert. Yet the intensity of her longing is no guarantee that water will be found. Whether there is water to be found has no bearing on

> When the wonder has gone out of a man he is dead. When all comes to all, the most precious element in life is wonder. Love is a great emotion and power is power. But both love and power are based on wonder. Plant consciousness, insect consciousness, fish consciousness, animal consciousness, all are related by one permanent element, which we may call the religious element in all life, even in a flea: the sense of wonder. That is our sixth sense. And it is the natural religious sense.
>
> D.H. LAWRENCE, *THE PHOENIX*

how she feels. A real longing for water does not mean that there is water to be found.

Yet this argument can become seriously misleading. It can easily be assumed that, precisely because this woman longs for water, there is no water to be found. The fact that she longs for something could be held to mean that, for that very reason, the water does not exist. All longings are thus declared to be illusory, breaking the hearts of those who experience them. If there is no water, then those who long for it are doomed to disappointment and bitterness.

The Great Projection Theory argues that, since there is no God in the first place, anyone who believes in God is deluded. So how are we to account for this delusion?

But why should there be no water, just because we long for it? Whether there is water in the desert depends purely and simply on whether there is water in the desert. We may long for that water, or we may regard it as a matter of total disinterest. Our attitude towards that water has no bearing on whether the water exists. Imagine a pool of water in that desert. Are we to believe that it will disappear, if someone admits to being thirsty? Or that it could not exist in the first place?

The argument began by suggesting that nothing exists simply because we would like it to exist. That is true. The existence of our thirsty desert traveller does not mean that pools of water must exist to slake her thirst. Yet the argument soon becomes more menacing, and loses its grip upon reality. It begins to assert that something cannot exist, if we want it to exist. It is here that the argument falls and fails. My experience of thirst does not mean that there is water nearby. Yet it certainly points to my need for water if I am to survive physically. Is not thirst a natural sign of our need for water, and hunger a natural sign of our need for food? So might not our sense of longing for something profound and satisfying also be a natural sign of a real human need – and a sign that something exists with the potential to satisfy that need?

Although we have skirted round the subject thus far, the argument was really devised to deal with God. The Great Projection Theory argues that, since there is no God in the first place, anyone who believes in God is deluded. Religious beliefs are 'illusions, fulfilments of the oldest, strongest and most urgent wishes of mankind. The secret of their strength lies in the strength of those wishes' (Sigmund Freud). So how are we to account for this delusion? How can we explain why so many people believe in a God, when (as a matter of plain fact) there is no such God? The answer lies in our tendency to project our longings, and draw the conclusion that they point to God. We believe in God because we want to believe in God – yet in reality we are deluded, because there is no God to believe in. We are real,

Atheism is as much a matter of faith as Christianity.

and our feelings are real; God is simply an improper and unjustified interpretation of those feelings.

Yet the Great Projection Theory is a double-edged sword which can wound those who use it as much as those against whom it is used. For the theory threatens to prove too much – that all our beliefs rest on hidden longings. If a belief rests on a longing, it could be argued that faith in God reflects nothing more than our longing that there should be a God. Yet it could be argued that a belief that there is no God rests on exactly the same basis – a hope and desire that this is, in fact, the case. Atheism is as much a matter of faith as Christianity. As Boris Pasternak, the author of *Dr Zhivago*, once remarked: 'I am an atheist who has lost his faith.' Might not atheism's basic assumptions rest on a longing for total autonomy, not having to give account to anyone, and not being limited by anything?

It is easy to imagine someone who might have excellent reasons for not wishing to believe that there is a God. Think of someone who commanded a liquidation squad during the Stalinist purges of the 1930s, or the commandant of a Nazi extermination camp during the Second World War. Such a person might well find the idea of God profoundly threatening. Suppose such a God might find his action in slaughtering large numbers of human beings absolutely repulsive, and choose to punish him in consequence? Might not such a person have a very good reason for hoping that there is no God? Having evaded retribution in the present life, the hope of having evaded it for ever clearly has considerable attraction.

The Great Projection Theory thus offers an explanation of any kind of religious belief – whether that belief involves the existence or non-existence of God. In addition, it contains at its heart what appears to be a fatal logical flaw – the assertion that something cannot exist if we wish it to exist.

As the Apostle Paul says, 'He is not far from any one of us, for in him we live and move and have our being.' Scripture also says, 'From him and through him and in him are all things.' If everything has its being in God, then apart from him how can the living live or the moving move? So the greatest human misery is to be separated from the one without whom it is impossible to exist in a truly human way. Of course, in one sense if we exist at all we are 'in' him. But if we have no knowledge of him, no understanding, no memory of or love for him, then we cannot really be said to be 'with' him. Our minds, made in the image of his mind, are so devoid of his memory that we cannot even be reminded what it is that we have forgotten.
AUGUSTINE OF HIPPO, *CONFESSIONS*

ST AUGUSTINE
Simone Martini (1284–1344)

But there is another factor which we have not even begun to explore. Christianity affirms that God created humanity. What if we are *meant* to want to relate to God? Might our sense of emptiness and lack of fulfilment be intended to point us to something or someone who could fulfil it? Might Augustine, perhaps the greatest Christian writer of late antiquity, have been right when he penned the following words as a prayer to God: 'You have made us for yourself, and our hearts are restless until they find their rest in you'?

4 Plato's Cave

Human nature longs for something worthwhile. There is a restlessness, a dissatisfaction with much of what we know and experience. Perhaps this is just the way things are, and we will have to get used to it. But this is not the only explanation of this situation. What if this restlessness is meant to make us seek for something that we have not yet found which would give us the rest and tranquillity which we do not yet know? Our desire for the good and the beautiful is real, yet can easily become attached to objects or experiences which betray it.

Our life on earth will at times point beyond itself, hinting at something beyond our vision.

If we were made for something greater than anything that earth can offer, we would expect two things to be true. In the first place, we should expect to find that nothing that is created or finite could ever really satisfy us. If we have been created to enjoy the riches of heaven, how can we ever be satisfied with what earth has to offer us? Thomas à Kempis, writing in the fourteenth century, once commented that 'the glory of the world fades away' in the light of thoughts like that.

Our birth is but a sleep and a forgetting;
The Soul that rises with us, our life's Star,
Hath had elsewhere its setting,
And cometh from afar:
Not in entire forgetfulness,
And not in utter nakedness,
But trailing clouds of glory do we come
From God, who is our home:
Heaven lies about us in our infancy!
Shades of the prison-house begin to close
Upon the growing Boy
But he beholds the light, and whence it flows,
He sees it in his joy;
The Youth, who daily farther from the east
Must travel, still is Nature's Priest,
And by the vision splendid
Is on his way attended;
At length the Man perceives it die away,
And fade into the light of common day.

Earth fills her lap with pleasures of her own;
Yearnings she hath in her own natural kind,
And, even with something of a Mother's mind,
And no unworthy aim,
The homely Nurse doth all she can
To make her Foster-child, her Inmate Man,
Forget the glories he hath known,
And that imperial palace whence he came…

O joy! that in our embers
Is something that doth live,
That nature yet remembers
What was so fugitive!…

Hence in a season of calm weather
Though inland far we be,
Our Souls have sight of that immortal sea
Which brought us hither,
Can in a moment travel thither,
And see the Children sport upon the shore,
And hear the mighty waters rolling evermore…

William Wordsworth,
Intimations of Immortality from
Recollections of Early Childhood

But in the second place, we should expect that our life on earth will at times point beyond itself, hinting at something beyond our vision. We may not be able to see it, but hints of its presence abound. The poet William Wordsworth wrote of living on the borderlands of experience, knowing that factors within our experience can be pointers to something lying beyond it.

We live in anticipation, not fulfilment. Experiences which we have on earth are hints of something greater which is yet to come.

We therefore live in anticipation, not fulfilment. Experiences which we have on earth can thus be seen as hints of something greater which is yet to come. If our real destiny lies with some good which lies beyond this world, we should expect to encounter hints of this goodness in this world. They will only be hints – yet they will be real, conveying to us something of what lies tantalizingly beyond us.

The overwhelming sense of joy that comes with achieving something worthwhile can thus be seen as a hint of something even more wonderful that is yet to come. On earth, such joy is transient, fading away with a speed which can frighten us as much as disappoint us. It seems so transient and brief. If we were to pursue such earthly joy for its own good, we would be doomed to frustration and bitterness. But what if such experiences of joy are not to be seen as things to be captured before they fade away, but as hints of a joy which we have yet to experience, something which awaits us?

The joy that we know on earth is like an anticipation of something greater. It would be like someone drawing aside a curtain, and allowing us a glimpse into the most wonderful of worlds. We long to enter in and explore it. Yet before we have had time to begin to take in its wonder, the curtain is pulled back again, and we lose it from sight. We have yet to enter into it, but we know that it is there and that it awaits us. It is thus a desire for something that we have never encountered in our experience, but which we feel we have begun to know, however poorly.

Thomas Aquinas, perhaps one of the greatest thinkers of the medieval period, argued that there was an analogy between the world and God. If God created the world, we should expect it to bear his likeness in some way. Just as an artist signs a picture, or the personal concerns of a composer are reflected in music, so the nature of God can be found echoed in the world. The creator is reflected in the creation. At times that reflection may be dim and perhaps somewhat distorted. Yet what we encounter on earth has the capacity to point beyond itself to something more glorious and satisfying. It is only a symbolic representation of the things that will truly satisfy, which, like the wind and moonbeams, can never

ST THOMAS AQUINAS READING
Fra Bartolomeo (1472–1517)

Meditation on God's works enables us, at least to some extent, to admire and reflect on God's wisdom. We are thus able to infer God's wisdom from reflection upon God's works. This consideration of God's works leads to an admiration of God's sublime power, and consequently inspires reverence for God in human hearts. This consideration also incites human souls to the love of God's goodness. If the goodness, beauty and wonder of creatures are so delightful to the human mind, the fountainhead of God's own goodness (compared with the trickles of goodness found in creatures) will draw excited human minds entirely to itself.
THOMAS AQUINAS,
SUMMA CONTRA GENTILES

be captured or preserved. Why be satisfied with a poor reflection, when the real thing has been both signified and promised?

This deep sense that the present world is little more than a shadow of something greater has haunted Western literature since the earliest of times. The analogy offered by Plato is perhaps the best known. Imagine a dark cave, in which a group of people have lived since birth. They know no other world. In the cave there is a fire burning, offering them both warmth and light. As the flames rise, they cast shadows on the walls of the cave. For those living in the cave, this world of flickering shadows is all that they know. Their grasp of reality is limited to this world. If there is a world beyond the cave, it is something which they do not know and cannot imagine. Their horizons are limited and determined by the shadows and half-light.

Now imagine that one of the group of people huddling around that fire discovers a secret way out of the cave. He slips away, unnoticed by the remainder of the group. As he explores the recesses of the cave, he stumbles across a passage, hidden in the living rock and unnoticed in the darkness. He begins to explore, slowly and tentatively moving forward and upwards. Finally, he emerges into glorious sunlight, entering into a world of fresh air, green trees, blue skies and radiant brightness. The world of flickering shadows has been left behind, and a new world discovered.

The flickering and gloomy world of the cave was real, not imaginary. Yet the reality of that world does not call into question the possibility that there might be another world – a world which is somehow hinted at or signposted by the

world we know. Our desire for something that seems never to be satisfied is one of those hints – a hint that ours is not the only world, and that true fulfilment is not to be found within it.

The desire that we experience in the world can thus be thought of as a real desire for something that lies beyond this world. It is hinted at by our experiences of the world, yet should not be attached to anything in the world. If we begin to think that our desire is really for a transient object or earthly experience, we shall be disappointed and frustrated. What really satisfies and fulfils is not those objects or experiences, but what they point to. They are images or reflections of what we desire and long for – but they are not in themselves that fulfilment. They are like wisps of smoke from a fire, curling upwards before being dispersed into nothingness by the wind. They are flickering shadows on the wall of a dark cave. Our desires have become attached to things that are little more than shadows, when they are meant to be attached to something which cannot decay or disappoint. The shadows have thus become the rivals of the true object of our desires.

Our desires have become attached to things that are little more than shadows, when they are meant to be attached to something which cannot decay or disappoint.

Perhaps in the darkness of that cave, we might rest satisfied with those shadows. They are, after all, better than

Our life is no dream, but it should and perhaps will become one.
NOVALIS

nothing. If there was nothing more to reality, then we would have to be satisfied with them. Yet our deep sense of a longing which is unquenched by our experiences in this world is a vital clue to the meaning of the universe. It is like the man who broke free from that cave, and discovered a brilliant and clear new world beyond it. It lifts the curtain, perhaps only briefly, on something else. Yet that glimpse, however brief, is enough to make us want more – and wonder how it may be identified, found and grasped.

5 Beauty Beyond Description

In the previous chapter, we encountered Plato's famous analogy of the twilight world of a dark cave, whose features were illuminated by the flames of a fire. It is a world of flickering shadows, which bears little relation to the real world of bright colours and fresh air. The analogy makes a powerful point, which has haunted human thinking ever since. Might not the world that we know be like that cave? The cave dwellers automatically assumed that the world they knew was the only world, unaware of a beautiful and fragrant world which lay beyond them.

It is easy for us to smile at their stupidity. Yet how could they have known otherwise? And might now we make precisely the same mistake? Suppose there is another world – either existing alongside our world, or a future reality which begins to break into the present. Might not we make precisely that same mistake? Our smiles at the delusion of primitive cave dwellers might well mask a deeper, yet comparable, delusion on our part – that we have fallen into the mistake of assuming that the world we know and experience is the only and therefore the best world. But what if there is another world, one whose beauty and joy eclipses all that we know?

The man who escaped from the cave would have experienced a world for which life in the cave could never have prepared him. His senses would be bombarded with sights, fragrances and sounds which were absent from the gloom of the underground cavern. How, then, could he communicate them to his fellow cave dwellers? If he were to return to the cave, how could he begin to describe what he had seen and heard to those who remained behind? How could he ever describe the brilliant blue sky to those who knew only the drab world beneath? Or the fragrance of pine trees by a salty sea to those who knew only the smell of stale smoke?

THE HUMAN CONDITION (1935)
René Magritte (1898–1967)

It is as hard to explain how this sunlit land was different from the old Narnia as it would be to tell you how the fruits of that country taste. Perhaps you will get some idea of it if you think like this. You may have been in a room in which there was a window that looked out on a lovely bay of the sea or a green valley that wound away among mountains. And in the wall of that room opposite to the window there may have been a looking glass. And as you turned away from the window you suddenly caught sight of that sea or that valley, all over again, in the looking glass. And the scene in the mirror, or the valley in the mirror, were in one sense just the same as the real one: yet at the same time they were somehow different – deeper, more wonderful, more like places in a story: in a story you have never heard but very much want to know. The difference between the old Narnia and the new Narnia was like that. The new one was a deeper country: every rock and flower and blade of grass looked as if it meant more. I can't describe it any better than that: if you ever get there you will know what I mean.

It was the Unicorn who summed up what everyone was feeling. He stamped his right fore-hoof on the ground and neighed and then cried:

'I have come home at last! This is my real country! I belong here. This is the land I have been looking for all my life...'

C.S. Lewis, *The Last Battle*

The only means at his disposal would be words – words through which he could try to convey his new experience in terms of experiences his audience would already know. He could have tried to describe the sky in its brilliant blue vastness or the sweetness of the fragrance of wild flowers using sights and odours which were already familiar. This description could never be fully achieved – but at least his audience would learn that there was a world to be discovered and worth discovering, and gain an inkling of what they would experience on entering into it.

One of the most haunting novels of André Gide (1869–1951) is *La Symphonie Pastorale*. The book is set in French-speaking Switzerland in the 1890s, and tells the story of the complex relationship between a Protestant pastor and Gertrude, a girl who has been blind from birth.

Our present world contains clues and signs to another world – a world which we can begin to experience now, but will only know in all its fulness at the end of things.

Of particular interest is the way in which the pastor tries to convey to Gertrude such things as the beauty of the alpine meadows, the brilliant colours of the alpine flowers, and the majesty of the snow-capped mountains. He tries to describe the blue flowers by the river in terms of the colour of the sky – only to realize that she cannot see the sky to appreciate the comparison. Throughout the work, he finds himself constantly frustrated by the limits of language to convey the beauty and wonder of the natural world to Gertrude. But words are the only tools he has at his disposal. He can only persevere, knowing that in this case a reality which can never be fully expressed in words can only be conveyed through those words.

Then a new and somewhat unexpected development occurs. An eye specialist in the nearby city of Lausanne indicates his belief that her condition is operable, and that her sight can be restored. After three weeks in the Lausanne nursing home, she returns to the pastor's home. She is now able to see, and experience for herself the sights which he had tried to convey using words alone. 'When you gave me

When I was a child, I spoke like a child, I thought like a child, I reasoned like a child; when I became an adult, I put an end to childish ways. For now we see in a mirror, dimly, but then we shall see face to face. Now I know only in part; then I will know fully, even as I have been fully known.
1 CORINTHIANS 13:11–12

back my sight,' she said, 'my eyes opened on a world more beautiful than I had ever dreamt it could be. Yes, truly, I had never imagined that the daylight was so bright, the air was so brilliant, and the sky was so vast.' The reality far exceeded the verbal description. The pastor's patient and clumsy words could never adequately describe the world she could now see for herself, which called out to be experienced rather than merely described.

For the Christian, our present world contains clues and signs to another world – a world which we can begin

to experience now, but will only know in all its fulness at the end of things. God created the world with these signs and markers already in place. There is an analogy, a likeness, between what we know and what is to come. It is this principle which underlies the parables told by Jesus – stories about things and events in this world which possess a remarkable ability to point beyond themselves to the kingdom of God. Stories about sheep, coins, seeds and houses become pointers to how our desires can find their final fulfilment. We shall explore one of these in the following chapter.

Nothing can fully prepare us for heaven, when it is finally encountered – except the thought that it is like the best of this world, only better.

Our sense of emptiness and longing now becomes something of immense significance. Instead of being simply an irritating aspect of human life, it becomes a clue. It is like an analogy, a parable in itself, pointing to a possible ending of that emptiness. The ending of that emptiness would take away its pain and put in its place something intrinsically worth possessing.

Although the analogies we find around us cannot fully prepare us for the full radiance and wonder of what lies to hand, they allow us to begin to build up a picture of what it is like. André Gide's pastor was able to help Gertrude appreciate at least something of what the world of colour would be like; yet she was taken aback by the gloriousness of that world when it suddenly became accessible. Perhaps nothing can fully prepare us for heaven, when it is finally encountered – except the thought that it is like the best of this world, only better.

6 The Pearl of Great Price

Anselm of Canterbury (1033–1109), one of the greatest thinkers of the Middle Ages, once wrote these words, in the form of a prayer: 'Lord, give me what you have made me want; I praise and thank you for the desire that you have inspired; perfect what you have begun, and grant me what you have made me long for.' Anselm here expresses the basic idea which we have been exploring: that, in some way, our longings and desires have their origins in God, and can only be fulfilled by God. Our sense of emptiness is thus not accidental, nor is it a spurious and meaningless irritation. It is a fundamental clue to our origin, purpose and destiny. Nothing that we experience on earth can truly satisfy. Yet this does not mean that we are condemned permanently to a state of restlessness and dissatisfaction. We have simply allowed our desires to become attached to objects or goals which cannot truly fulfil them. Our disappointment is all the greater because we had dared to hope that, this time, we might really have found

> *Our sense of emptiness is not accidental – it is a fundamental clue to our origin, purpose and destiny. Nothing that we experience on earth can truly satisfy.*

My light, you see my conscience,
because, 'Lord, before you is all my desire',
and if my soul wills any good, you gave it to me.
Lord, if what you inspire is good,
or rather because it is good, that I should want to love you,
give me what you have made me want:
grant that I may attain to love you as much as you command...
Perfect what you have begun,
and grant me what you have made me long for,
not according to my deserts but out of your kindness
that came first to me.

ANSELM OF CANTERBURY

something that brings fulfilment. We need to fix our desires upon something that can truly satisfy.

Perhaps one of the greatest challenges to our imaginations is to think of something which exceeds in beauty anything that we have ever experienced. Part of the challenge lies in identifying the most wonderful thing that we have ever encountered. We are then asked to imagine something that would surpass even this.

Many are able to point to a moment in their lives which has supreme significance. Everything led up to that point, and then away from it. The experience in question is a defining moment. Someone might consider falling in love

to have been the most fulfilling and worthwhile experience of their life. Another might consider it to be the moment she discovered a major new scientific fact, or noticed a pattern in her observations which enabled a new scientific discovery. A third person might consider his defining moment to be his experience of coming across a beautiful paradise island for the very first time, and being entranced by its unspoilt splendour.

Each of these experiences is real and important. Yet they are to be seen as pointers, indicating an analogy between the temporary joy and fulfilment that we experience on earth and the more profound and permanent fulfilment that we can have by knowing God. This does not

mean that our earthly joys and hopes are to be seen as foolish, or things we should condemn. Good though they are, they pale into insignificance compared with the greater joy that is had through knowing God. This theme can be seen at many points in the New Testament. Perhaps the most moving statement of the wonder of knowing God can be seen in Paul's letter to the Christians in the Roman colony of Philippi. After listing all his achievements, Paul comments on how they are all trivial compared with the unsurpassable richness of knowing Christ: 'Whatever was to my profit, I now consider loss for the sake of Christ. What is more, I consider everything a loss compared to

ST PAUL
Italian School (eighteenth century)

the surpassing greatness of knowing Christ Jesus my Lord' (Philippians 3:7–8). These words resonate with the excitement of discovery and fulfilment. Paul had found something that ended his long quest for truth and meaning.

THE PEARL OF GREAT PRICE *Domenico Fetti (1589–1624)*

Jesus made a similar point in one of his parables. He compared the kingdom of heaven to a pearl of great price. 'The kingdom of heaven is like a merchant looking for fine pearls. When he found one of great value, he went away and sold everything he had and bought it' (Matthew 13:45–46). The merchant finds a priceless pearl for sale, and decides that he will sell everything in order to possess it. Why? Because here is something of supreme value. Here is something which is worth possessing. Everything else he possesses seems of little value in comparison.

The merchant searching for that pearl is himself a parable of the long human search for meaning and significance. It is clear from the parable that he already possesses many small pearls. Perhaps he bought them in the hope that they would provide him with the satisfaction that he longed for. Yet he is still looking for something really special – and when that comes along, he gladly sells them all in order to take hold of it.

Many of the beliefs and values that we take hold of are like those lesser pearls. They seemed worthwhile, and for a time offered fulfilment. Yet, deep down, we knew that there had to be something better. The accumulation of possessions does not bring happiness. Neither does the acquisition of status and power. These are like drugs with the power to soothe and console for a while, before their power begins to wane. We begin to look around again, seeking something which will achieve permanently what these goals promised for a time.

When the merchant found that pearl of great price, he gladly abandoned all that he had accumulated. Here, at last, was something that was worth possessing!

> A monk in his travels once found a precious stone and kept it. One day he met a traveller, and when the monk opened his bag to share his provisions with him, the traveller saw the jewel and asked the monk to give it to him. The monk did so readily. The traveller departed, overjoyed with the unexpected gift of the precious stone that was enough to give him wealth and security for the rest of his life. However, a few days later he came back in search of the monk, found him, gave him back the stone, and entreated him, 'Now give me something much more precious than this stone, valuable as it is. Give me that which enabled you to give it to me.'
>
> ANTHONY DE MELLO

What he had obtained previously was a preparation for this final purchase. He had come to know the true value of what he possessed, and was looking for the final culmination of his search for a precious pearl. When he saw it, he knew that everything already in his possession was dull and lacklustre by comparison. Just as the brilliance of the sun drowns that of the stars, so that they can be seen only at night, so this great pearl allowed the merchant to see what he already owned in a different light. What he had thought would satisfy him proved only to disclose his dissatisfaction, and make him long for something which was, for the moment, beyond his grasp. And then he saw that special pearl. He knew he had to have it.

THE RICH FOOL

In the previous chapter, we considered the parable of the pearl of great price. It is fascinating to set this alongside the parable of the rich fool (Luke 12:15–21). In this parable, we read of a highly successful farmer, whose fields provide a rich and abundant harvest. Not satisfied with what he already possesses, he decides to tear down all his existing storehouses, and replace them with bigger and better ones. Then he will have found fulfilment! Yet that night, the rich fool dies. The only ones who benefit from his scheming are his heirs.

The parable makes the point that we should throw our energy and commitment into something that will last. The rich fool believed that money and possessions would give him security and peace of mind. He said to himself: 'You have lots of good things laid up for many

THE RICH MAN BEING LED INTO HELL
David Teniers the Younger (1610–90)

And he said to them, 'Take care! Be on your guard against all kinds of greed; for one's life does not consist in the abundance of possessions.' Then he told them a parable: 'The land of a rich man produced abundantly. And he thought to himself, "What should I do, for I have no place to store my crops?" Then he said, "I will do this: I will pull down my barns and build larger ones, and there I will store all my grain and my goods. And I will say to my soul, Soul, you have ample goods laid up for many years; relax, eat, drink, be merry." But God said to him, "You fool! This very night your life is being demanded of you. And the things you have prepared, whose will they be?" So it is with those who store up treasures for themselves but are not rich towards God.'
LUKE 12:15–21

years. So take things easy! Eat, drink and be merry!' Yet in the end, those possessions did nothing of the sort. Jesus made this point with the following words: 'Do not store up for yourselves treasures on earth, where moth and rust destroy, and where thieves break in and steal. But store up for yourselves treasures in heaven' (Matthew 6:19–20). Instead of looking for something that is as transitory as the grass in the field, we should be looking for something that is going to stay with us and continue to satisfy us for ever. Everything that the rich fool amassed had to be left behind.

Oscar Wilde once defined a cynic as 'a man who knows the price of everything and the value of nothing'. The rich fool was well aware of the price of his possessions; he assumed that their price guaranteed their value. Yet the most radical question which anyone can be asked is not how much their possessions cost, but whether they have found something of value – that is, something that makes living worthwhile.

The conclusion Jesus draws from the parable is simple: human life 'does not consist in an abundance of possessions'. It is more than this. Someone could gain the world, yet lose his reason for living. After all, which of Jesus' disciples was the richest? Judas was the one who earned thirty pieces of silver – a huge sum of money in those days – for betraying Jesus. Unable to live with the guilt of what he had done, he took his own life. The money could not compensate. He had gained riches, but had turned his back on the one who really mattered.

THE TREACHERY OF JUDAS
Giotto di Bondone (c.1266–1337)

With that in mind, let us return to the parable of the pearl of great price. As we saw, this parable invites us to think of something that is both costly and wonderful – so wonderful that it exceeds everything in beauty and radiance. Yet the pearl was not merely of great value, intrinsically worth possessing; it was also costly. How are we to possess something so precious, when it is something we cannot hope to purchase or acquire? It is like promising a beggar

How are we to possess something so precious, when it is something we cannot hope to purchase or acquire?

happiness, if only he can afford rich food and sumptuous accommodation.

Perhaps our lot is like that of a different merchant – one who has seen this great pearl, and realizes that all he owns is drab and grey in comparison, yet cannot do anything about it. Before seeing the pearl, he was content with his lot. But there seems to be nothing he can do about it. He is like a man trapped in a cave, enviously listening to another describe a world which exceeds his dreams. Now he knows

that he is living in the shadows, and yearns for something better. But he cannot escape. A better world may exist; it would seem, however, that he is trapped where he is.

There is little comfort in the thought of something wonderful which lies permanently beyond our means and reach. What hope does that bring? Surely all that this thought brings in its wake is sadness at the realization that we can never possess such a wonderful thing, or enter into such a wonderful country. It is like being allowed a glimpse of the promised land across the River Jordan, catching its subtle fragrance, yet not being allowed to enter it. At this moment, the heart's desire is disclosed, yet not fulfilled, leaving us sadder than before. It is as if the thought of something better causes an unspeakable desire to rise within us, crying that there must be more – and that we will not rest until we enter it and possess it.

That might seem to be the end of the matter. In fact, it is only the beginning.

8 The Lost Sheep

The deep sense of desire in human nature is often expressed in terms of mystic and distant lands, such as El Dorado or Shangri-La. These often become a focus for our longing for a better world than that which we know, and which we long to enter and possess.

Imagine that some such wonderful kingdom did indeed exist, which exceeded anything that this world can offer in terms

> Why should a man be scorned, if, finding himself in prison, he tries to get out and go home? Or if, when he cannot do so, he thinks and talks about other topics than jailors and prison-walls? The world outside has not become less real because the prisoner cannot see it.
>
> J.R.R. Tolkien, 'On Fairy Stories'

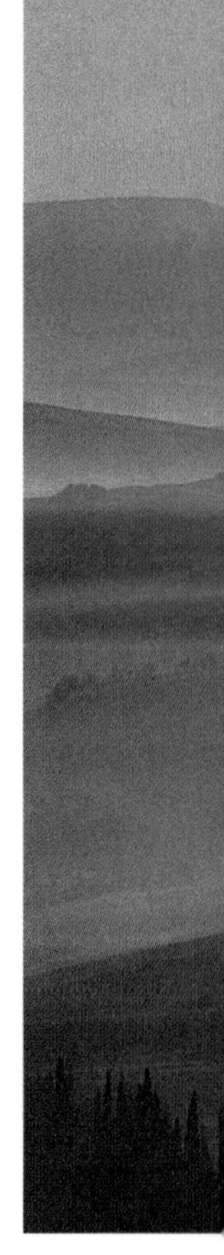

of its beauty and peacefulness. It is a world from which pain, evil and suffering have been banished. It is like the best that this world can offer, without the pain and sadness which are so tragic an aspect of our present existence. Imagine that world, in all its wonder, and savour its attraction.

This was the situation faced by the people of Israel, as they neared the end of their forty years of wandering through the wilderness. Israel gathered on the borders of Canaan, longing to enter into the land which had been promised to their forebears. It was to be 'a land flowing with milk and honey'. The hope of entering it had sustained them for a generation. They prepared to cross the River Jordan, and enter into what they had longed and waited for over the years. The

The object of our longing exists and will indeed fulfil our deepest longings. Yet we are cut off from it.

PIAZZA D'ITALIA
Giorgio de Chirico (1888–1978)

> Which one of you, having a hundred sheep and losing one of them, does not leave the ninety-nine in the wilderness and go after the one that is lost until he finds it? When he has found it, he lays it on his shoulders and rejoices. And when he comes home, he calls together his friends and neighbours, saying to them, 'Rejoice with me, for I have found my sheep that was lost.'
> LUKE 15:4–6

land they had longed for was finally within reach.

But what if the land could not be reached? What if there was a vast chasm, a huge gorge, between Israel and the promised land, which could not be bridged? What if that promised land was raised up on a high plateau, surrounded by sheer cliffs which could not be climbed by human beings? What if the land is real – yet completely beyond our grasp? If this is so, that land becomes a symbol of frustration and despair. Our longing to enter it heightens our pain as we realize that we simply cannot do this. We would be like Tantalus in the ancient Greek legend, who had success snatched from him when it was within his grasp.

The simple fact is that we are separated from the object of our longing. That object exists, and will indeed fulfil our deepest longings when we encounter it. Yet we are cut off from it. It is like being lost, and unable to find our way home. One of Jesus' most moving parables concerns a lost sheep. This sheep became separated from the others, strayed from the safety of the fold and could not find its way home. Jesus tells how the shepherd went out in search of that lost sheep, and carried it home. Presumably the sheep was tired, perhaps even injured, and could not make

God chose to come to where we are. Instead of expecting us to find him, he comes to us.

its way home on its own. The concern of the shepherd for his sheep was such that he carefully put the sheep over his shoulder, and brought it home to safety.

Notice how the shepherd went to where the lost sheep was, and carried it home. This is a powerful picture, and allows us to introduce one of the most wonderful of all religious ideas. Using the technical vocabulary of the Christian faith, we are speaking of the idea of 'incarnation'. In plain English, we are talking about a God who comes to be where we are, in order to take us to this promised land. The doctrine of the incarnation declares that God enters into our human situation, sharing its sorrows and griefs, in order to take us into the promised land in which there is no sorrow, pain or crying. We could not get there on our own. But the king of that land chooses to come and fetch us, and welcome us into the kingdom – just as the shepherd carried his lost sheep home to the fold.

One of the most basic teachings of Christianity is that God chose to come to where we are. Instead of expecting us to find him, he comes to us. Some people think of religion as being like climbing up a ladder to find God. Yet Christianity affirms that God chose to come down that ladder to meet us, and then to bring us home rejoicing.

9 A Royal Invitation

To explore this theme further, let us return to the image of a lost sheep. It had strayed from the security of the fold, and was unable to get home. Perhaps it had been injured, and could not manage to walk. Or perhaps it had fallen into a hole in the ground, and could not escape. Ideas such as 'being lost', 'being injured' and 'being trapped' are of major importance to understanding our situation as human beings.

The human dilemma is that we are trapped in a situation from which we cannot escape. A whole series of images is used in the Bible and the Christian tradition of biblical interpretation to describe this predicament. It is like being trapped in a sea of mud; our every movement and attempt to escape causes us to sink deeper. It is like being in a pit, whose walls are too high for us to climb. It is like being seriously ill, and not having access to healing medicines. It is like being in prison, with no hope of escape, or being lost in the dark, unable to find our way

It is of little value to be told that we are trapped in a pit; we need someone to get us out.

THE VOICE OF THE LORD
James Tissot (1836–1902)

home. It is about being in a situation which prevents us from achieving our dreams, and from which we are unable to free ourselves.

We need someone to deliver us. It is of little value to be told that we are trapped in a pit; we need someone to get us out. It is not particularly helpful to learn that we are imprisoned, and cannot escape; we need someone to rescue us by throwing open the door and leading us to safety. We are indeed separated from the object of our desire. But what can be done to bring us home? Who can open the gate and allow us to enter the promised land?

It is at this point that Christianity proclaims its good news – that deliverance and freedom are to hand. The Christian gospel (the word literally means 'good news') begins to develop the great theme of redemption. Jesus Christ is not just a good religious teacher – who might be able, for example, to tell us what we need to do to live well. He is our saviour – someone

The bonds of death encompassed me
and destructive torrents overtook me,
the bonds of Sheol tightened about me,
the snares of death were set to catch me.
When in anguish of heart I cried to the Lord
and called for help to my God,
he heard me from his temple,
and my cry reached his ears.
PSALM 18:4–6

who rescues us from our predicament. Our situation is so serious that we are unable to deliver ourselves, and need someone from outside our situation to save us. Jesus is the one who delivers his people from their sin and its effects. At Christmas, Christians recall the gospel accounts of the birth of Jesus, and the great emphasis placed on the fact that he is to deliver us. Thus Joseph is told that Mary will give birth to a son, and that he is to be named 'Jesus', because he will save his people from their sins (Matthew 1:21).

Patiently I waited for the Lord;
he bent down to me and listened to my cry.
He raised me out of the miry pit,
out of the mud and clay;
he set my feet on rock
and gave me firm footing.
On my lips he put a new song,
a song of praise to our God.
PSALM 40:1–3

Yet this redemption will mean little to us unless we realize our need for deliverance and trust that Jesus is indeed able to provide that deliverance. Christianity sets out a rich understanding of both the nature of our predicament, and the deliverance which is offered to us through the death and resurrection of Jesus. That deliverance is like being led into glorious freedom after years of captivity in a gloomy dungeon. It is like being restored to full health after a long and serious illness, which at times seemed as if it was incurable.

The image of people dwelling in a gloomy cave, whose

We are not being tantalized by a vision of a wonderful world which we cannot ever hope to see, know or enter. We are invited to enter as esteemed guests.

darkness is illuminated only by the flickering of a fire, may help us explore this point further. Suppose we think ourselves into their situation, recognizing that this is the only world that they know, and the only world that they believe to exist. Suppose that someone were to come to them from a world outside that cave – a world of which they have no knowledge, even if it may figure in their dreams and hopes. Suppose that this person were able to tell them something of this other world, using language and images with which they were familiar to describe it. We have already given some thought to how this could be done.

We were not made to rest in this world. It is not our true native land.
FATHER ANDREW SDC, *IN THE SILENCE*

Now we need to introduce a completely new element into our thinking. The inhabitants of the cave are trapped in their gloomy and shadowy world. To tell them that near at hand but out of reach there exists a brilliant world of fresh air and space would only increase their sense of misery. That other world might be real – but it could not be theirs. They are doomed to remain prisoners of that cave, unable to break free from its confinement. But suppose the visitor were not merely a messenger from the world beyond the cave. What if he were the only person who could deliver them from the darkness and shadows, and lead them into the brilliant light of the world beyond? What if he were like the shepherd come to bring the sheep home to where it really belonged?

This is the essence of the Christian understanding of the significance of Jesus. Through his teaching, Jesus sets out a vision of the kingdom of God. Through his death and resurrection, he makes it possible for us to enter this kingdom as privileged and welcome guests of its king. We are not being tantalized by a vision of a wonderful world which we cannot ever hope to see, know or enter. We are invited to enter this world, not as those who have blundered in as unwelcome intruders, but as the esteemed guests of its lord. More than that; the lord of that world has entered into our world to issue the invitation, and accompany us to the feast which has been prepared for us.

10 The Unknown God

We saw earlier how Plato's analogy of the cave points to a world which lies beyond our present experience. For Plato, the human quest for beauty, truth and goodness could be explained in terms of our attempt to reach beyond the limitations of our world to a transcendent world lying beyond it, of which we could know something in the present. Yet it seems a cold and very impersonal world – a shadowy world of ideas.

There is a world of difference between knowing an idea and knowing a person.

This was certainly the view of the great French thinker Blaise Pascal (1623–62). On his death, a scrap of paper was found sewn inside his shirt. On it were written the words: 'The God of Abraham, the God of Isaac and the God of Jacob, not of philosophers and scholars.' By this, he meant that he longed for (and had found) a living personal God, rather than the abstract and remote idea of God favoured by philosophers. The American philosopher Paul Elmer Moore once wrote of 'the loneliness of an ideal world without a Lord'. He longed for the impersonal world of

'Men of Athens, I have seen for myself how extremely scrupulous you are in all religious matters, because, as I strolled round looking at your sacred monuments, I noticed among other things an altar inscribed: To An Unknown God. In fact, the Unknown God you revere is the one I proclaim to you.

'Since the God who made the world and everything in it is himself Lord of heaven and earth, he does not make his home in shrines made by human hands. Nor is he in need of anything, that he should be served by human hands; on the contrary, it is he who gives everything – including life and breath – to everyone. From one single principle he not only created the whole human race so that they could occupy the entire earth, but he decreed the times and limits of their habitation. And he did this so that they might seek the deity and, by feeling their way towards him, succeed in finding him; and indeed he is not far from any of us, since it is in him that we live, and move, and exist, as indeed some of your own writers have said: We are all his children.

'Since we are the children of God, we have no excuse for thinking that the deity looks like anything in gold, silver or stone that has been carved and designed by a man.

'But now, overlooking the times of ignorance, God is telling everyone everywhere that they must repent, because he has fixed a day when the whole world will be judged in uprightness by a man he has appointed. And God has publicly proved this by raising him from the dead.'

ACTS 17:22–31

Platonic ideals to disclose a face, a person – someone to whom he could relate. There is a world of difference between knowing an idea and knowing a person.

This theme can be seen in one of the most important early confrontations between Christianity and classical paganism, found in the apostle Paul's speech to the philosophers of first-century Athens (recorded in Acts 17:16–34). Paul, who had discovered Christianity some years earlier, set about travelling throughout the eastern Mediterranean region, telling his audiences about his discovery and its implications. One of the cities in which he spoke was Athens, the home of the 'Academy', the famous philosophical institution established by Plato centuries earlier. In the ancient world, Athens seems to have gained a reputation for its interest in novelty, and it is entirely possible that some of those who gathered to hear Paul did so simply because what he had to say was new.

Paul opened his address by noting that the Athenians were noted for their religiosity. They were aware of the spiritual dimensions of life, and as concerned as anyone to find out the meaning of life. Yet it was clear that

ST PAUL PREACHING IN ATHENS
Raphael (1483–1520)

there were questions which they could not answer. Paul drew attention to an altar which he had seen at Athens inscribed with the words 'to an unknown god'. Whoever had constructed the altar was clearly aware of some deity who could not be named. They were aware of a presence within themselves and nature, but did not know who or what it was.

In his address, Paul argues that he is able to identify this nameless and faceless god. 'What you worship as something unknown, I proclaim to you.' Paul argued that he was able to name what the Athenians believed to lie permanently beyond their grasp. This theme of 'making the face of God known' pervades the New Testament. The word which is usually translated as 'revelation' has the basic meaning of 'removing a veil, so that the face may be seen'. For Paul, there is a personal presence at the heart of the cosmos, who has created us so that we may enter into a relationship with him. This is not a barren idea, but a personal reality who may be known, loved and named.

There is no doubt that the Greeks knew of a spiritual thirst, and longed for its quenching – even if they did not know how this might come about. One of the best-known Orphic texts is found in the Petelia

You will find a well-spring on the left of the House of Hades
And by its side a white cypress tree
Do not approach this spring
But you will find another by the Lake of Memory
There is cold water flowing from it
And there are guardians attending it.
Say: 'I am a child of the earth and starry heaven
But my race is of heaven alone. You know this yourselves.
And see, I am parched from thirst, and I am dying.
Give me quickly that cold water which flows from the Lake of Memory.'
And they will give you to drink of that holy well-spring
And you will reign with other heroes.
PETELIA TABLET

What if that 'unknown god' chose to come and find us? What if he chose to come to where we are – in space, time and history?

tablet; it clearly points to a hope and longing of this kind.

In it we find a powerful statement of a real thirst, and the hope for a well of cooling water to quench that thirst permanently. It is a symbol of the human condition. But who could satisfy it? Perhaps the 'unknown god' was the one to whom they looked in hope, wondering who this god was and what he might do. Paul's proclamation that this god was near to hand must have electrified them.

There are many today who are aware of a spiritual dimension to reality. The crude old materialist dogmas

which asserted that there was nothing beyond or in addition to the physical side of life seem tired and outdated to many. In their place, there is a new awareness of the spiritual dimension of life, and a longing to find its fulfilment. Many are aware of a 'sense of divinity' within themselves or in nature. Those same ideas are found in the writings of classical philosophy, particularly Stoicism. Yet this spiritual reality is often conceived of as an impersonal force. For Paul, this unknown spiritual reality is a personal and living God who can be known, not merely known about – and who seeks us out, rather than requires us to find him.

It is this theme of a God who can *and wants to* be known that is of especial interest. The Athenians honoured 'an unknown god'. Yet what if that 'unknown god' *chose* to make itself known? We so often hear about 'the human quest for God'. But what if that God chose to come and find us? What if he chose to come to where we are – in space, time and history? What if he offered to give us that which we have been searching for, but have never found?

11 The Precious Gift

The man stood in the marketplace, offering to give away banknotes to those who passed by. Some rushed past, anxious not to get involved. It was probably illegal, or some kind of trap. Others looked at him pityingly, thinking him mad. At the end of the afternoon, the man had as many banknotes as when he had begun. He put the perfectly genuine banknotes into his wallet, and returned home. It was the same every time he tried it. People were convinced that there was something wrong with him or the money he was trying to give away. Nobody in their right mind would give away something so valuable.

For some, the act of giving something away suggests that it is not valuable in the first place. Who in their right mind is going to give away something precious? People usually give away things for two reasons: either those things are cheap and lack any real value, or they expect to get something back in return – something which exceeds the value of what they give away.

God's gift is not simply precious; it is healing, and brings us to the fulfilment and wholeness which is his desire for us.

One of the most remarkable aspects of the Christian gospel is the idea of grace. Two ideas which might thus seem to be in conflict are thus asserted to be true at one and the same time. The invitation to life offered by the gospel is declared to be costly, perhaps beyond anything we could ever imagine. Yet it is being offered to us as a free and gracious gift.

God had no need to suffer so laboriously, but man needed to be reconciled thus.
ANSELM OF CANTERBURY

Why are we so suspicious of this? We have become hardened to the idea of generosity, suspecting that there is some concealed condition which converts a gift into a demand.

Yet it is important to appreciate that there is another way of viewing the giving of precious gifts. A gift is a demonstration of love. And while many are reluctant to quantify something as important as love, there is no doubt that many believe that the greater the love of one for another, the more precious the gift that may be given as a token of that love. The pearl of great price is not simply something which is intrinsically worth possessing. It is also a demonstration of the love of the giver for the one who receives it.

HAGAR GIVING ISHMAEL WATER FROM THE MIRACULOUS WELL IN THE DESERT
Charles-Paul Landon (1760–1826)

Early Christian writers compared the gospel to a food which satisfied hunger; a cooling spring of water which quenched the deepest of thirsts; a love which reached out and embraced the most despised and rejected of people; a salve for the wounds of human nature. God's gift is not simply precious; it is healing, and brings us to the fulfilment and wholeness which is his desire for us. It is he who made humanity long for him, and in fulfilling that desire, he is bringing humanity to its true and intended fulfilment.

We have spoken of the costliness of what God so graciously gives without considering why this should be so.

Why should this healing and fulfilment be so costly and precious? The value of something can be spoken of in two different ways. In the first place, we can speak of the value of what it achieves. For someone who is seriously ill, the value of a medicine lies in what it effects. The drug in question may only cost a few cents, yet it is able to save a life. The fulfilment which the Christian gospel offers is itself something of enormous value. It is something that nothing finite or created can provide, and for that reason alone is priceless. Money simply cannot purchase the happiness which human nature longs for.

Yet there is another way of considering the value of a gift – the cost to the giver. The costliness of a gift cannot always be measured in material terms. The price of a precious ointment might be measured in terms of the number of hours which it takes to manufacture, or the cost of its raw materials. The cost of some gifts is to be counted in terms of human life. Sometimes people have to die so that others might live. This brings us to the core of the Christian faith – the crucifixion of Jesus.

To appreciate the meaning of the crucifixion is to draw close to the banks of the River Jordan, and catch a glimpse of the promised land that lies beyond – knowing that, this time, the means of entry lies to hand.

The astonishing revelation of Calvary is in part that man's actions are so gigantic and irreparable as to require the death of God himself to put them right.
M.C. D'ARCY, *DEATH AND LIFE*

12 The Secret of the Kingdom

At first sight, thinking about a man who was put to death on a cross 2,000 years ago might seem a highly unpromising starting point for anything. Why should an ancient execution concern us today?

It is clear from contemporary evidence that crucifixion was a widespread form of execution within the Roman empire at the time of Jesus. The victim was generally flogged or tortured beforehand, and then might be tied or nailed to the cross in practically any position. This form of punishment appears to have been employed ruthlessly to suppress rebellions in the Roman provinces, such as the revolt of the Cantabrians in northern Spain, as well as those of the Jews. Josephus, a Jewish historian, provides us with accounts of the crucifixion of Jewish fugitives who attempted to escape from besieged Jerusalem at the time of its final destruction by Roman armies, which make horrifying reading. In the view of most Roman jurists, notorious criminals had to be crucified on the exact location of their crime, so that 'the sight may deter others

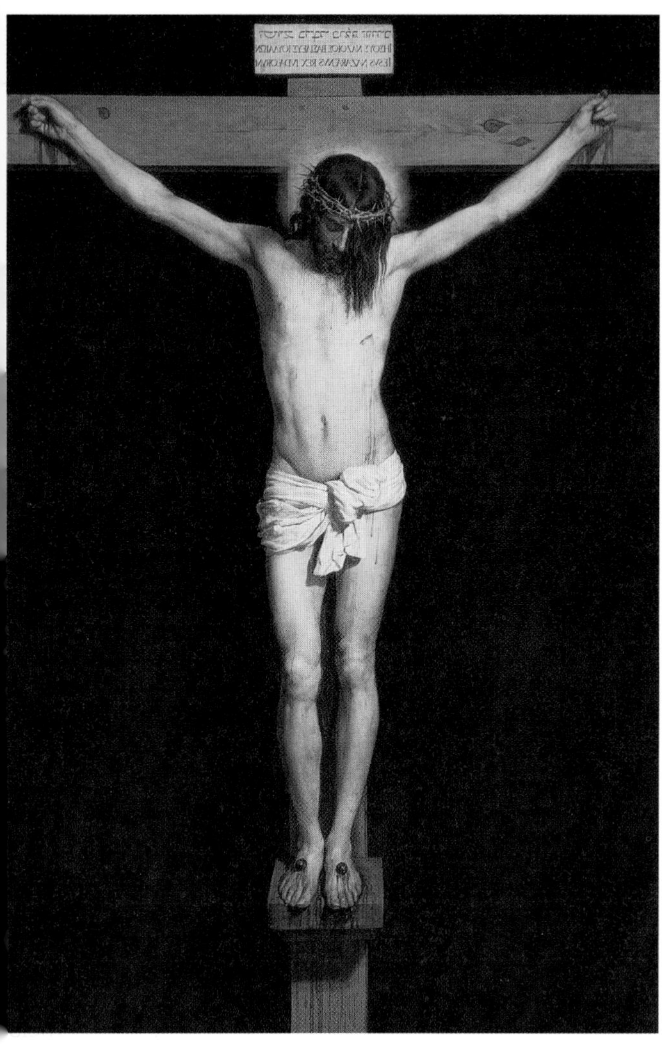

THE CRUCIFIXION
Diego Rodriguez de Silva y Velázquez (1599–1660)

from such crimes'. Perhaps for this reason, the Roman emperor Quintillian crucified criminals on the busiest thoroughfares in order that the maximum deterrent effect might be achieved.

It is therefore little wonder that the pagan world of the first century reacted with disbelief and disgust to any suggestion that Jesus might hold – or be – the key to the meaning of life. Crucifixion was a punishment reserved for the lowest criminals, clearly implying that Jesus belonged to this category of people. How could his death have any relevance for the culturally and intellectually sophisticated society of the day? Or of our own day and age?

Crucifixion was a punishment reserved for the lowest criminals. How could Jesus' death have any relevance for our own day and age?

Yet we must draw a distinction between the event and its deeper meaning. Often a hidden significance lies beneath the surface of events. The stolen glance between lovers; the carefully chosen words in a conversation whose meaning is discerned only by those who are in the know; both are examples of hidden meanings, missed by the crowd yet discerned by the few. The cross is like a parable, a mystery, whose true meaning must be grasped before it can open the door to all that it promises. Rightly understood, what at first seems to be nothing more than a symbol of suffering and death becomes the gateway to the promised land of the kingdom of God.

What are parables? For some, a parable is just an analogy. Yet the full meaning of the word 'parable' includes the idea of 'mystery', 'secret' or 'riddle'. Jesus explained his use of parables to the disciples when he told them that 'the secret of the kingdom of God has been given to you. But to those on the outside everything is said in parables' (Mark 4:11). The meaning of the parable is not self-evident. It is hidden. It needs to be explained, so that the secret of the kingdom of God can be uncovered.

Earlier, we looked at the parable of the lost sheep. For one listener, that might seem to be nothing more than a story about a shepherd who loses and then finds a sheep. These things happen all the time. So what is so special about the story? That listener might shrug his shoulders, and walk away. Nothing special there.

Yet another might realize that the parable was a window into the nature and workings of a God who loved a wayward people so much that, when they got lost or injured, he came and found them and brought them home. The parable is then a wonderful affirmation of the amazing love of God, and a comforting reassurance of the presence of a caring and compassionate God in the complexities of life.

Both listeners heard the same story. Yet they discerned very different things. The same is true of the cross. Imagine two people, watching Jesus

> The fact of Jesus coming is the final and unanswerable proof that God cares.
> WILLIAM BARCLAY

Christ die upon the cross on that first Good Friday, all those years ago. One might see nothing more than an everyday execution of an unimportant Jew. The other might see the saviour of the world dying, in order that the world might be saved. One sees Jesus as a criminal dying for his own sins. The other sees him as the Son of God, dying for all our sins. Each observer sees the same event; they place very different interpretations upon it. They both *see* the same event; they *discern* very different things.

Another example may help explain this important point. In 49BC, Julius Caesar crossed a small river with a legion of soldiers. That river was called 'the Rubicon', and it marked the boundary between Italy and Cisalpine Gaul, a colonized region to the north-west of Italy in modern-day France. As an event, it was not especially important. The Rubicon was not a great river, and there was no particular difficulty in crossing it. Yet the political significance of that event was enormous. For a Roman army to cross this frontier was a deliberate act of

rebellion against Rome. By doing this, Caesar was declaring war against Rome. Some might see only an army crossing a river; those who knew more discerned the implications of that event, and realized it was a declaration of war.

> I do not try, Lord, to attain your lofty heights, because my understanding is in no way equal to it. But I do desire to understand your truth a little, that truth that my heart believes and loves. For I do not seek to understand so that I may believe; but I believe so that I may understand. For I believe this also, that 'unless I believe, I shall not understand'.
>
> ANSELM OF CANTERBURY

In many ways, the death of Jesus can be said to be like Caesar's crossing of the Rubicon. The event itself appears unexceptional, except to those who know its hidden and deeper meaning. The Rubicon was a small river, and it was not difficult to cross. People have crossed much wider rivers before and since then. As an event, it hardly seems significant. Similarly, Jesus died upon a cross. Everyone has to die sometime. On the basis of contemporary records, we know that an incalculable number of people died in this way at that time. Jesus was not alone in being executed in this way. As an event, the crucifixion hardly seems important or noteworthy – unless there is a deeper meaning.

This leads to a very significant conclusion. It is possible to observe the event of the crucifixion, without being aware of the meaning of the cross. Two people may be in the same position, and yet see something quite different, as the following lines by Frederick Langbridge (1849–1923) make clear:

> Two men look out through the same bars:
> One sees the mud, and one the stars.

Langbridge asks us to imagine two people in prison, looking out through the same window. Although they share the same vantage point, they nevertheless see very different things. The point that Langbridge makes is that some people see nothing but the rut of everyday life, ending in death, while others raise their eyes to heaven, knowing that their ultimate destiny and fulfilment lies with God. Their situation is identical; their outlooks are totally different.

The New Testament affirms that beneath the publicly observable death of Jesus on the cross lies a hidden meaning, grasped only by some.

The New Testament affirms that beneath the publicly observable death of Jesus on the cross lies a hidden meaning, grasped only by some. When that meaning is grasped, a totally new perspective on life is opened up. The word 'faith', as used in a Christian context, can be thought of as grasping this deeper meaning, and entering into a new way of life on its basis.

We must now turn to explore this deeper meaning, and the images which the New Testament uses to convey it to us.

13
The Ransom

The question we must address in unlocking the meaning of the cross is similar to that faced by the unfortunate inhabitants of Plato's cave. How can the brilliance, radiance and freshness of the world beyond that cave ever be communicated to those who know nothing other than the gloomy flickerings inside their cavern? How can the fragrance and beauty of the outside world be communicated using only the shadow-language of the cave? How can the world of spiritual reality ever be described in terms of our own ordinary world of everyday experience?

> *Just as the human eye cannot cope with the brilliance of the sun, so the human mind cannot cope with the full glory of God.*

The richness of spiritual reality is like a strong wine, which has to be diluted if we are to be able to handle it. Many early Christian writers compare understanding God with looking directly into the sun. The human eye is simply not capable of withstanding the intense light of the sun. And just as the human eye cannot cope with the brilliance of the sun, so the human mind cannot cope with the full

glory of God. Spiritual reality has to be accommodated to our capacity to handle it.

That issue is of decisive importance in relation to the deeper meaning of the cross. That meaning – which transcends in its fulness and wonder anything we know or can imagine – has to be conveyed in terms of ideas, situations and images which we already know. These allow us to gain an insight into the full meaning of the cross – but can never convey that meaning in all its fulness. The New Testament thus offers us a powerful series of pictures which allow us insights into the meaning of the cross. They are like snapshots of the promised land, hints of the glory of the kingdom of God. Each demands to be savoured and studied slowly, as if it were a fine vintage wine.

One of the most important and helpful pictures is that of a 'ransom'. This image is of especial importance to Christians, as it is used on the lips of Jesus himself, who declared that he came 'to give his life as a ransom for many' (Mark 10:45). The image is also found elsewhere in the New Testament: 1 Timothy 2:5–6 speaks of Jesus Christ being a 'mediator between God and humanity... who gave his life as a ransom for all'.

To appreciate the richness of this image, let us carry out a thought experiment. Imagine that you come from a rich family, and have cherished a lifelong ambition to visit the island of Sicily. On your arrival, you happily begin to explore its many Roman archaeological sites and its beautiful yet rugged landscape. You become impatient with the regular tourist guides, and decide that you will explore the island by yourself. On the second day of this adventure, you are confronted by two men, one of whom is carrying a shotgun. They invite you to share their humble hospitality, while arrangements are made to transfer a suitably large sum of money to secure your release.

You realize that you have been kidnapped, and that there is nothing that you can do about it. Your emotions are a complex mixture of anger, guilt and fear. How could you have allowed yourself to get into this situation? And will you ever get out? Try to think yourself into this situation, and appreciate the sense of helplessness and hopelessness that goes with it. Whether you get out of it depends totally on someone else being prepared to pay a ransom for you. Your life is in their hands. What happens if the folks back home would be glad to be rid of you? As day after day passes, you sink into despair.

Now try to imagine the sense of utter relief and delight you would experience if the news came through that your family had ransomed you. You would be free! And (perhaps just as important) you would have mattered enough to your family for them to pay the price that was demanded.

A ransom is a price that is paid to achieve someone's freedom. In the Old Testament, the emphasis falls especially upon the idea of being freed, of liberation, rather than speculation about the nature of the price which was paid to achieve this liberation. Thus Israelites who were liberated from exile in Babylon are often referred to as the 'ransomed of the Lord' (Isaiah 35:10).

The picture of a 'ransom' suggests three fundamental ideas. First, it speaks of someone who is held in captivity, almost certainly against their will. One might think of a prominent Sicilian citizen who has been kidnapped by the Mafia. The fundamental theme is that someone is trapped in a situation in which they do not want to be – and from which they cannot extricate themselves. Left to their own devices, they have no hope of deliverance.

For God so loved the world that he gave his only Son, so that everyone who believes in him may not perish but may have eternal life.
JOHN 3:16

This leads on to the second idea prompted by the image of a 'ransom' – that of a price which is paid to bring about the freedom of the captive. The more valuable the person being held to ransom, the greater the price demanded. One of the most astonishing things about the love of God for us is that God was prepared to pay so dearly to set us free. The price of our freedom was the death of his one and only Son. How much we must matter to this God if the price which is paid to redeem us is so great!

One of the most astonishing things about the love of God for us is that God was prepared to pay so dearly to set us free.

And thirdly, the image of 'ransom' points to the great theme of liberation – being set free from captivity. The New Testament is saturated with the good news of freedom from the power of sin and death. We have been set free to enjoy the 'glorious freedom of the children of God' (Romans 8:21). Christ's death on the cross throws aside the barriers which prevented us from finding our fulfilment with God.

LAMENT OF CHRIST BY THE VIRGIN AND ST JOHN
Peter Paul Rubens (1577–1640)

A similar set of ideas is associated with the image of 'redemption'. The basic theme is that of 'being bought back', which underlies the practice of redeeming slaves, a familiar event in New Testament times. A slave could redeem himself by buying his freedom. The word used to describe this event could literally be translated as 'being taken out of the forum' (the slave market). As with the idea of ransom, we are dealing with the notion of restoring someone to a state of liberty. Captivity is set to one side, and a new life and lifestyle is opened up.

The deeper meaning of the cross which these images present to us is that of something which allows us to break free from our imprisonment to achieve our true destiny and find our true fulfilment in God. The image casts light on three fundamental issues. It tells us that we are indeed trapped in a prison – but that liberation is possible! The cost of that liberation has been borne by none other than God, who longs for us to enter into the life which he has prepared and purposed for us. We are being asked to say 'Yes!' to this offer of transformation.

Those who dwell in the flickering shadows of the cave are thus promised, not merely that there *is* a better world, but that it awaits us. We do not need to remain in the shadows, hoping for a better tomorrow. A new world awaits us, and invites us to enter.

I have a dream that one day every valley shall be exalted, every hill and mountain shall be made low, the rough places will be made plains, and the crooked places will be made straight, and the glory of the Lord shall be revealed, and all flesh shall see it together...

And when we allow freedom to ring, when we let it ring from every village and every hamlet, from every state and every city, we will be able to speed up that day when all of God's children, black men and white men, Jews and Gentiles, Protestants and Catholics, will be able to join hands and sing in the words of that old Negro spiritual, 'Free at last! Free at last! Thank God Almighty, we are free at last!'

MARTIN LUTHER KING,
CONCLUDING WORDS OF THE 'I HAVE A DREAM' SPEECH, 28 AUGUST 1963

14 The Divine Healer

To help us understand the meaning of the cross, we need to explore one further image – the image of 'salvation'. This term is used frequently in the New Testament. The verb 'to save' is often used in the future tense, suggesting that salvation should be thought of at least in part as a future event – something which is still to happen in all its fulness, although it has begun to happen in the present. The idea is that something has been inaugurated in the present, but will reach its fulfilment in the future. A seed has been planted and has begun to grow; its final flowering, though assured, has yet to happen. Salvation thus refers to both a present reality and a future hope. But what sort of reality and hope?

Salvation refers to both a present reality and a future hope. But what sort of reality and hope?

The associations of 'salvation' include deliverance, preservation, or rescue from a dangerous situation. The verb is used by writers outside the New Testament to refer to being saved from death by the intervention of a rescuer, or to being cured from a deadly illness. The word 'salvation'

THE DELIVERY OF ISRAEL OUT OF EGYPT
Samuel Colman (1780–1845)

is used in this sense by the Jewish historian Josephus to refer to the deliverance of the Israelites from Egyptian bondage. Earlier, we noted how the theme of deliverance is of major significance in relation to the image of 'ransom'. 'To be saved' refers to being rescued or delivered from a dangerous situation, just as the Israelites were delivered from their captivity in Egypt at the time of the Exodus. In much the same way, Christ is understood to deliver humanity from the fear of death and the penalty and power of sin. The name 'Jesus' means 'God saves'; it is clear that the New Testament understands this to mean 'saves from sin'. We are reminded of this each time we hear the Christmas story: 'You are to give him the name Jesus, because he will save his people from their sins' (Matthew 1:21). Christ's death is the means by which the penalty due for sin is paid – a penalty which we could not hope to pay ourselves – and the doorway to eternal life and fulfilment is thrown open.

The biblical understanding of 'salvation' is enormously rich, and also includes the ideas of 'wholeness' or 'health'. When someone who has been ill is healed, he or she is restored to their former state of health and wholeness. The creation stories of Genesis make it clear that God created humanity in a state of wholeness, and that this wholeness was subsequently lost. Just as healing involves restoring someone to health, so salvation involves restoring believers to wholeness, to the state in which we were first created by God.

The gospel of Jesus, then, is about spiritual healing. In many respects the gospel is like a medicine – something which heals us, even though we do not

> Look once again to Jesus Christ in his death upon the cross. Look and try to understand that what he did and suffered he did and suffered for you, for me, for us all. He carried our sin, our captivity and our suffering, and did not carry it in vain. *He carried it away.* He acted as the captain of us all. He broke through the ranks of our enemies. He has already won the battle, our battle. All we have to do is to follow him, to be victorious with him. Through him, in him we are saved. Our sin no longer has any power over us. Our prison door is open... When he, the Son of God, sets us free, we are *truly* free.
>
> KARL BARTH

fully understand how it works. Faith in this gospel can make us whole, by restoring us to fellowship with God, and beginning the long and painful process of learning to live with God and for God. Why should it be painful? Because we have tried to live without God for so long that when we finally come to make room for him, we find it very difficult to make the adjustment. Many of us know only too well what happens when the blood circulation is restored after it has been cut off from an arm or leg. It can be acutely painful, as the limb tries to readjust to the presence of the life-giving fluid. Yet that pain comes about through the limb coming to life again. So it is with coming back to God: it is painful, but it is also coming back to life.

Just as healing involves restoring someone to health, so salvation involves restoring believers to wholeness, to the state in which we were first created by God.

In order to appreciate this aspect of the cross properly, let us try out another thought experiment, focusing on the idea of healing and restoration. Imagine that you have now left the hospitality of your Sicilian kidnappers. While you were in captivity, you were badly scratched by some undergrowth as you were forced to march to your place of captivity. Now things have become worse; ominous dark lines are beginning to appear in your upper arm. As soon as you can, you seek medical advice. The situation turns out to be very serious: you have blood poisoning. In earlier times, this would have been fatal.

There was no cure before the invention of certain crucial drugs in the twentieth century.

Think yourself into the situation in which you know that you are seriously ill – and there is nothing that can be done about it. You will die of blood poisoning. Being confronted with the thought of death is not pleasant or easy, and gives rise to a jumble of emotions

Coming back to God is painful, but it is also coming back to life.

including fear and sadness. Take some time to think yourself into this difficult situation, and try to experience the sense of despair that accompanies it.

Now take this a stage further. You learn that a new drug has been developed which can heal you and restore you to health. Try to imagine the sense of excitement and anticipation which you would feel. The drug is rumoured to be very expensive. Yet it works. It has the potential to heal you and others who are in similar situations. Suddenly, despair begins to lift, and hope dawns in its place. You are just as ill as you were before – but a new element has entered into the situation, which gives you hope where before there was none.

Now we take this to its final stage. The drug has arrived. Its cost has been met by your anxious family. Yet it will not benefit you in the slightest while it remains in its sterile container. It must be administered to you, whether by mouth or injection. You must receive the drug into your system, so that it can begin its healing work. While the drug remains in its container, it merely has the potential to heal. You will not be healed by knowing that a cure is available; that knowledge by itself is not enough. Nor will you be healed if the drug is brought into your presence. It must be taken and applied. Then healing can begin.

The bread of life will only satisfy your hunger if you feed on it.

The point being made here is simple. It is one thing to read the New Testament, and realize that, in the view of its writers, Jesus has the potential to transform the human situation. There is also a need for what the philosopher Kierkegaard called 'an appropriation process of the most passionate inwardness'. In other words, if we are to benefit from the spiritual healing Jesus has to offer, we need to make him part of us through faith. As Jesus himself says in

The thing is to understand myself, to see what God really wishes me to do; the thing is to find a truth which is true for me, to find the idea for which I can live and die. What would be the use of discovering so-called objective truth, of working through all the systems of philosophy and of being able, if required, to review them all and show up the inconsistencies within each system; what good would it do me to be able to develop a theory of the state and combine all the details into a single whole, and so construct a world in which I did not live, but only held up to the view of others; what good would it do me to be able to explain the meaning of Christianity if it had no deeper significance for me and for my life; what good would it do me if truth stood before me, cold and naked, not caring whether I recognized her or not, and producing in me a shudder of fear rather than a trusting devotion? I certainly do not deny that I still recognize an imperative of understanding... but it must be taken up into my life, and that is what I now recognize as the most important thing. That is what my soul longs after, as the African desert thirsts for water. That is what I lack, and that is why I am left standing like a man who has rented a house and gathered all the furniture and household things together, but has not yet found the beloved with whom to share the joys and sorrows of his life.

Søren Kierkegaard

the gospel of St John, the bread of life will only satisfy your hunger if you feed on it (John 6).

To understand the full wonder of the gospel at this point, we need to consider the costliness of the drug which has been prescribed for us. Jesus died, so that we might live. Jesus suffered pain and suffering on the cross, so that people might finally be set free from their wounds. We have already seen how the human quest for fulfilment is grounded in a desire for none other than God himself. The immense joy which comes from finding our fulfilment reminds us that this is indeed a 'pearl of great price'.

> If you confess with your lips that Jesus is Lord and believe in your heart that God raised him from the dead, you will be saved. For one believes with the heart and so is justified, and one confesses with the mouth and so is saved. The scripture says, 'No one who believes in him will be put to shame.' For there is no distinction between Jew and Greek; the same Lord is Lord of all and is generous to all who call on him. For, 'Everyone who calls on the name of the Lord shall be saved.'
> ROMANS 10:9–13

Yet the pearl is priceless in another respect. It is not simply that the joy of divine fulfilment overshadows everything that money can buy. It is that Jesus had to die in order to make that fulfilment possible. The most precious gift in the world required the death of the son of God himself. Yet he died willingly in order that we might have the joy of coming to life, and being healed from our wounds.

But Christians believe that Jesus did not merely die upon the cross; he rose again from the dead. As we will see in the next chapter, the resurrection of Jesus is an integral aspect of the comfort and joy of the Christian faith.

15 The Dawn of New Life

The question we face in trying to understand the riddle of life is whether there is something beyond this world which allows us to make sense of what we experience in the present. So once more, we return in our thoughts to the cold, damp and dark cave, watching its inhabitants shivering as they huddle around the fire for warmth. Around them, the shadows can be seen flickering on the walls. Many are wondering whether there is another world, beyond the confines of the cavern in which they are trapped. It is a theme that is often discussed, in hushed tones. But nobody really knows. Perhaps there is indeed another world beyond the cave, a great beyond which has yet to be discovered. But no one has been there, and come back to tell the tale.

There are some who claim to have come close to escaping. Some assert that they drew very close to a mystical gate, on the other side of which a wonderful landscape seemed to stretch for miles, beckoning them to enter. But they were unable to enter into that land, and return to bring others news of its sights and smells, or proof that they had been there in the first place. There have been too many false dawns, too many spurious reports of what lies beyond. Nobody really knows. Only someone who has been to that great beyond and returned to tell the tale is to

Only someone who has been to that great beyond and returned to tell the tale is to be trusted.

'Suppose we *have* only dreamed, or made up, all those things – trees and grass and sun and moon and stars and Aslan himself. Suppose we have. Then all I can say is that, in that case, the made-up things seem a good deal more important than the real ones. Suppose this black pit of a kingdom of yours *is* the only world. Well, it strikes me as a pretty poor one. And that's a funny thing, when you come to think of it. We're just babies making up a game, if you're right. But four babies playing a game can make a play-world which licks your real world hollow. That's why I'm going to stand by the play-world. I'm on Aslan's side even if there isn't any Aslan to lead it. I'm going to live as like a Narnian as I can even if there isn't any Narnia.'
C.S. LEWIS, *THE SILVER CHAIR*

All these died in faith. Although they had not received the things promised, yet they had seen them far ahead and welcomed them, and acknowledged themselves to be strangers and aliens without fixed abode on earth. Those who speak in that way show plainly that they are looking for a country of their own. If their thoughts had been with the country they had left, they could have found opportunity to return. Instead, we find them longing for a better country, a heavenly one. That is why God is not ashamed to be called their God; for he has a city ready for them.
HEBREWS 11:13–16

be trusted. Then others will follow in their footsteps.

Many today are fascinated by 'near-death experiences'. For many, the ideas of those who have come close to dying are endued with special spiritual qualities. They have drawn close to eternity, and perhaps caught a glimpse of something that they think lies beyond. They have then reported their experiences to others, and excited them with those reports. They seem to offer that elusive key to the mystery of death. Many who have had these near-death experiences have found them to transform their lives completely, persuading them that there is some greater spiritual reality almost within their grasp, which is profoundly worth pursuing.

Yet there is a difficulty here. All those who have such experiences have survived them. We are not talking about an experience of death and what lies beyond, but simply of drawing near to them. Whatever has been seen has been seen from a distance. If there is a world beyond death, it has at best been a glimpse of something seen from afar. Perhaps that glimpse was like the vision of the

TRIPTYCH OF THE DAY
Gaetano Previati (1852–1920)

promised land enjoyed by Moses – a genuine sight of a real promised land, but seen from across the River Jordan. Moses would not himself enter that land, but he was able to die knowing that it was within the grasp of those who would follow him.

But it might not be like that. It might be a dream, a delusion based on a hope rather than grounded in reality. 'Near-death experiences' might rest on nothing more than a trick of the mind as it loses consciousness. It would be comparable to a cave dweller who longed for a world beyond the flickerings and shadows, and whose longings slowly became indistinguishable from his experience. The longing became the reality, even when that reality was nothing more than a consoling dream.

Jesus journeyed through death, in order to lead us through that same death to the glorious world that lies beyond.

But what if someone were really to die, and return? What if someone were to enter into a realm that lies beyond, and return to take us with him into this new and wonderful realm? With this question, we come to the centrality of the resurrection of Jesus.

New Testament writers stress the reality of both Jesus' death and resurrection – obvious, for example, in Paul's great summary statement: 'For what I received I passed on to you as of first importance: that Christ died for our sins according to the Scriptures, that he was buried, that he was raised on the third day according to the Scriptures, and that he appeared to Peter, and then to the Twelve [disciples]' (1 Corinthians 15:3–5). Notice the emphasis on death, burial and resurrection. Paul's language makes it clear that he is solemnly passing on to others what he himself had once received. In other words, this is not something that he invented, but something that he had been entrusted with.

Jesus made his journey through death, in order to lead us through that same death to the glorious world that lies beyond. So we journey in hope, not in despair or anxiety. The person who has had a 'near-death experience' cannot be sure that she really has entered a new world; nor, even more importantly, can she know that she will be a welcome presence in whatever lies beyond. The New Testament

NOLI ME TANGERE
In the style of Mantegna

On this mountain the Lord of Hosts will prepare
a banquet of rich fare for all the peoples,
a banquet of wines well matured,
richest fare and well-matured wines strained clear.
On this mountain the Lord will destroy
that veil shrouding all the peoples,
the pall thrown over all the nations.
He will destroy death for ever.
Then the Lord God will wipe away the tears
from every face,
and throughout the world
remove the indignities from his people.
ISAIAH 25:6–8

offers us something profoundly more affirming and wonderful. Not only has Jesus burst through the barrier of death, so that we need no longer fear it, but he invites us to become 'citizens of heaven' through trusting in him. Not only has he been there, not only can he take us there, but we will be welcomed there – not as illegal immigrants or trespassers, but as welcome guests of honour in what lies beyond.

As we prepare to close this chapter, let us savour the image of a feast. It is a favourite biblical image for the kingdom of God, combining the elements of being in the company of great people, rejoicing, being refreshed and nourished, and being welcomed. That same image is used as the New Testament draws to its close, to affirm that those who trust in Jesus and draw near to him will feast with him in heaven (Revelation 19:9).

This theme of hope is of such importance that we shall explore it further in what follows.

16 Living in Hope

One of the greatest themes of the Christian gospel is that of eternal life. This is often misunderstood to mean something like 'an infinite extension of things'. The real meaning of the term, however, is much more profound. It means 'a new quality of life, which is begun now and will be consummated in the future, which nothing – not even death – can destroy'. 'Eternal life' is all about entering into a new quality of life here and now, in the full assurance that this new life will develop and grow. It is about relating to a wonderful, loving personal God – not an idea, but a person. God is someone who we can know, not simply know about. Above all, God is one who loves us and who we can love in return.

God is someone who we can know, not simply know about. Above all, God is one who loves us and who we can love in return.

Jesus himself affirmed that the love of God is like the love of someone who lays down his life for his friends (John 15:13). In the picture of someone laying down his life – giving his very being – for someone he loves, we have a powerful, striking and moving statement of the full extent of the love of God for us. We can call to mind the scene of Jesus Christ trudging in pain to Calvary, there to die for those he loved. He did not need to do this; he chose to do it. God does not simply love us; he demonstrates that love to us in action.

THE PROCESSION TO CALVARY
Ridolfo Ghirlandaio (1483–1561)

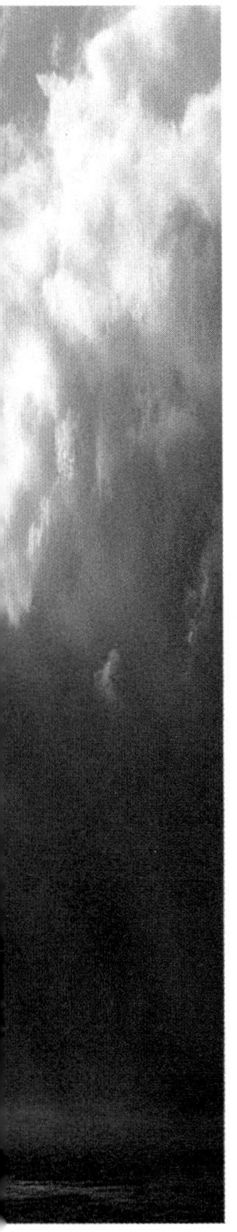

In the midst of an immense and frightening universe, we are given meaning and significance by the realization that the God who called the world into being, who created us, also loves us and cares for us, coming down from heaven and going to the cross to prove the full extent of that love to a disbelieving and wondering world – including ourselves.

The God who called the world into being loves us and cares for us – coming down from heaven and going to the cross to prove the full extent of that love to a disbelieving and wondering world.

Perhaps one of our greatest fears is coming to value someone so much that we cannot bear to be parted from them. Yet this fear does not hold us back from loving others and being loved in return. As Tennyson put it:

> 'Tis better to have loved and lost
> Than never to have loved at all.

One of the reasons why death is so distressing is that it separates us from those we love. It takes most of a lifetime to get to know someone fully. To have that person taken away from us leaves a void which is difficult to fill. Yet to love God, and to be loved by God, is something which nothing can destroy or remove. Even death itself merely casts aside whatever final barriers there may be to coming to God fully and totally.

This is one of the most important aspects of the Christian understanding of hope. 'Hope', sadly, is a word which has lost much of its meaning. For most, the word means little more than an expression of a faint-hearted belief we have little reason to believe will be fulfilled, as in: 'I hope the weather will improve.' The Christian sense of the word, however, has a very different tone. Hope, in its properly Christian sense, means a sure and confident expectation that what has been promised to us will finally blossom in all its wonderful glory. It is a strong and positive theme, affirming the reliability and

> The Christian hope is the hope which has seen everything and endured everything, and has still not despaired, because it believes in God. The Christian hope is not hope in the human spirit, in human goodness, in human endurance, in human achievement; the Christian hope is hope in the power of God.
> WILLIAM BARCLAY,
> *THE LETTER TO THE ROMANS*

> *Loving God and being loved by God are things of supreme value and worth, which will remain for ever.*

trustworthiness of the God who makes promises to us.

All of us need something reliable, unshakeable and secure on which to build our lives. There is little point in building our lives on a set of values or beliefs which will go out of date in five years. God is precisely such an unshakeable and immovable foundation for our lives. As we read in the book of Psalms, God is like a rock, a fortress and a strong tower – someone in whom we

> At bottom, everything depends upon the presence or absence of one single element in the soul – hope. All the activity of man, all his efforts and all his enterprises, presuppose a hope in him of attaining an end. Once kill this hope and his movements become senseless, spasmodic and convulsive, like those of someone falling from a height.
> HENRI FRÉDÉRIC AMIEL, *AMIEL'S JOURNAL*

find security, stability and peace. For the Psalmist, God is a consoling and caring presence and strength, even in the darkest moments of life as we walk through the valley of the shadow of death (Psalm 23:4). For the writers of the New Testament, loving God and being loved by God are things of supreme value and worth, which will remain for ever. As Paul put it:

> I am convinced that neither death nor life, neither angels nor demons, neither the present nor the future, nor any powers, neither height nor depth, nor anything else in all creation, will be able to separate us from the love of God that is in Christ Jesus our Lord (Romans 8:38–39).

For Paul, 'to live is Christ, and to die is gain' (Philippians 1:21). His personal relationship with God in

Jesus was something he treasured above everything else, and which he knew would remain with him for ever. He had found something which alone was fulfilling, which alone satisfied – and which would and could never be taken away from him.

17 The End of All Our Longing

We began our exploration in this book by looking at human desire – a desire for something which nothing within the world ever seems able to satisfy. As we explored the implications of this, we saw how this emptiness within human nature is a clue to the true meaning of the world. It is like a curtain being drawn aside for a moment, to give us a tantalizing glimpse of a distant and beautiful land, leaving us with a painful longing to enter into it.

When all is said and done, we are being asked to imagine, then to discover, and then to enter, a world which exceeds in beauty and wonder anything that we have known.

This book has set out an answer to the riddle of human longing, which has been found deeply satisfying by millions of men and women down the ages. This answer involves the recognition that our desire is secretly for something which lies beyond this world, yet which is mediated through the things of this world. That desire can become falsely attached to what we find in the world. Yet our experience of disappointment

For the garden is the only place there is, but you will not find it
Until you have looked for it everywhere and found nowhere that
is not a desert;
The miracle is the only thing that happens, but to you it will not
be apparent,
Until all events have been studied and nothing happens that you
cannot explain;
And life is the destiny you are bound to refuse until you have
consented to die.

Therefore, see without looking, hear without listening, breathe
without asking:
The Inevitable is what will seem to happen to you purely by
chance;
The Real is what will strike you as really absurd;
Unless you are certain you are dreaming, it is certainly a dream
of your own;
Unless you exclaim – 'There must be some mistake' – you must
be mistaken.

W.H. AUDEN, FROM 'ADVENT'

challenges this attachment, and invites us to discover the true object of our desire.

So what is this true object of our longing? How can we find it? For the Greeks, there was an 'unknown God' who was beyond knowing. Yet for the New Testament, this God has chosen to make himself known. The 'pearl of great price', which is supremely worth possessing, has been purchased for us through the death of Jesus. The 'bread of life', which alone has the power to satisfy our longings for

CHRIST SERVED BY ANGELS
Baldassare Franceschini
(1611–89)

meaning and immortality, has been made known to us – and revealed as a gift which is freely offered to us. The salve which will heal our wounds is ready and available.

Perhaps we are like Gertrude in André Gide's novel. Perhaps we have heard words used to describe aspects of the Christian faith – such as 'redemption' or 'heaven'. Perhaps we have heard attempts to describe the delight and satisfaction which come from knowing God. Will our eyes open on a world more beautiful than we could ever dream? For, when all is said and done, we are being asked to imagine, then to discover, and then to enter, a world which exceeds in beauty and wonder anything that we have known. If the creation delights us so much, how much more so will the one who created it.

The French philosopher Blaise Pascal argued that the human quest for happiness and fulfilment reflected an unacknowledged human longing for God, which was grounded in the simple fact that we are *meant* to relate to God. Human longings for

Let him keep the rest,
But keep them with repining restlessness.
Let him be rich and weary, that at last,
If goodness lead him not, yet weariness
May toss him to my breast.

GEORGE HERBERT, FROM 'THE PULLEY'

fulfilment and despair over apparent meaninglessness make sense in the light of our true desire being for God, even if we fail to realize that this is the case.

> What else does this longing and helplessness proclaim, but that there was once in each person a true happiness, of which all that now remains is the empty print and trace? We try to fill this in vain with everything around us, seeking in things that are not there the help we cannot find in those that are there. Yet none can change things, because this infinite abyss can only be filled with something that is infinite and unchanging – in other words, by God himself. God alone is our true good.

In the end, only God can satisfy – precisely because we are made to relate to God, and luxuriate in his presence.

For Pascal, there is a God-shaped emptiness within us, which only God can fill. We may try to fill it in other ways and with other things. Yet one of the few certainties of life is that nothing in this world satisfies our longing for something that is ultimately beyond this world. 'If we attempt to hold desire for the infinite within the narrow limits of the finite, if we love a thing or a fair face as if it could give us God, then the poor thing we have chosen ends by crumbling beneath our eyes, and leaves nothing behind in the fingers but a little pinch of dust' (Jean Mouroux). In the end, only God can satisfy – precisely because we are made to relate to God, and luxuriate in his presence.

Until we do so, our hearts will remain restless, and we must live with the pain of this desire and longing. Perhaps the image of exile captures this complex intermingling of desire, anticipation and memory. We are like people who have been taken captive from a land we know and love, and who long to return. Yet we have been ransomed from that captivity, and have the assurance that we shall return. That thought can only refresh and excite us. We need not be prisoners of this world of time and suffering. The passing beauty and joys of the world point us towards another

I saw a new heaven and a new earth, for the first heaven and the first earth had vanished, and there was no longer any sea. I saw the Holy City, new Jerusalem, coming down out of heaven from God, made ready like a bride adorned for her husband. I heard a loud voice proclaiming from the throne: 'Now God has his dwelling with mankind! He will dwell among them and they shall be his people, and God himself will be with them. He will wipe away every tear from their eyes. There shall be an end to death, and to mourning and crying and pain, for the old order has passed away!'
REVELATION 21:1–4

world, a New Jerusalem in which 'there will be no more death or mourning or crying or pain, for the old order of things has passed away' (Revelation 21:4). In the meantime, we must live and work in the world. Yet we do so as people who know that they are on their way home, and anticipate the joy of return and arrival.

In the end, there are basically two attitudes that we can adopt to life. We can see it as meaningless, something which has no real purpose. In this case, the most that we can hope for is to make the best of it while we can, trying to help others less fortunate than ourselves and distract ourselves from the fact that it is all pointless. Or we can see life as a glorious gift, something that is good in itself – yet which points to something even more wonderful that is yet to come. Even in this life, hints of this promised future break in, allowing us to anticipate what lies ahead. There *is* life beyond the cave – life more wonderful than we dared to hope for.

Other books by Alister McGrath

Christian Theology: An Introduction (Blackwell)

The Foundations of Dialogue in Science and Religion (Blackwell)

Science and Religion: An Introduction (Blackwell)

The Intellectual Origins of the European Reformation (Blackwell)

Jesus (Inter-Varsity Press)

Understanding the Trinity (Kingsway)

Making Sense of the Cross (Inter-Varsity Press)

Text acknowledgments

Bible extracts on pages 39, 50, 57, 87 and 98 are taken from the New Revised Standard Version of the Bible, Anglicized Edition, copyright © 1989, 1995 by the Division of Christian Education of the National Council of the Churches of Christ in the United States of America, and are used by permission. All rights reserved. Bible extracts on pages 60, 61, 102, 106 and 121 are taken from the Revised English Bible with the Apocrypha copyright © 1989 by Oxford University Press and Cambridge University Press. The Bible extract on page 66 is taken from the New Jerusalem Bible © 1985 by Darton, Longman & Todd Ltd and Doubleday & Company, Inc.

Page 43: Extract from *The Prayers and Meditations of St Anselm*, pages 93–94, translated by Sister Benedicta Ward, SLG, Penguin Classics, 1973. Copyright © Benedicta Ward, 1973. Reproduced by permission of Penguin Books Ltd.

Page 117: 'Advent' by W.H. Auden, from 'For the Time Being', *Collected Poems*, published by Faber and Faber Ltd (UK) and Random House, Inc. (US). Reproduced by permission.

Picture acknowledgments

Page 6: Rocks in the sea: Tony Stone Images.
Page 9: *The Antique Dealer*, by Heinrich Ede (1819–85): SuperStock Ltd.
Page 15: Mountain range: Telegraph Colour Library.
Page 16: *Paradise*, from a Book on the Seven Wonders of the World (miniature): Bibliothèque Royale de Belgique, Brussels/Bridgeman Art Library, London/New York.
Pages 18–19: Sand Dune: Phillip Ritterman/The Image Bank, 1998.
Page 25: *St Augustine*, from a polyptych, c.1320 (egg tempera and gold on panel), by Simone Martini (1284–1344),: Fitzwilliam Museum, University of Cambridge/Bridgeman Art Library, London/New York.
Page 29: *St Thomas Aquinas Reading*, c.1510–11 (fresco), by Fra Bartolomeo (1472–1517): Museo di San Marco dell'Angelico, Florence/Bridgeman Art Library, London/New York.

Page 31: Cave opening onto rock: James Casebere/The Image Bank, 1998.
Page 35: *The Human Condition* (1935) (oil on canvas), by René Magritte (1898–1967): Norfolk Museums Service (Norwich Castle Museum)/ Bridgeman Art Library, London/New York/copyright © ADAGP, Paris and DACS, London 1999.
Pages 38–39: The Matterhorn: Images Colour Library.
Pages 44–45: Sun through trees: Images Colour Library.
Page 45: *St Paul*, c.1730, by Italian School (eighteenth century): Phillips, The International Fine Art Auctioneers/Bridgeman Art Library, London/New York.
Page 46: *The Pearl of Great Price*, by Domenico Fetti (1589–1624): SuperStock Ltd.
Page 49: *The Rich Man Being Led into Hell*, by David Teniers the Younger (1610–90): copyright © The National Gallery, London.
Page 51: *The Treachery of Judas*, by Giotto di Bondone (1266–1337): SuperStock Ltd.
Page 52: Iguazu Falls: The Image Bank.
Page 55: Tuscany: Images Colour Library.
Page 56: *Piazza d'Italia* (oil on canvas), by Giorgio de Chirico (1888–1978): Art Gallery of Ontario (Gift of San and Ayala Zacks, 1970), Toronto/Bridgeman Art Library, London/New York/copyright © DACS 1999.
Page 60: *The Voice of the Lord*, by James Tissot (1836–1902): SuperStock Ltd.
Page 62: Stairway to light archway: Mary Heller/The Image Bank, 1998.
Page 67: *St Paul Preaching in Athens*, by Raphael: The Ancient Art and Architecture Collection.
Page 69: Rocks: copyright © Shooting Star/Photonica.
Page 70: Lake Mohonk: Julie Mihaly/The Image Bank, 1998.
Page 73: *Hagar Giving Ishmael Water from the Miraculous Well in the Desert*, by Charles-Paul Landon (1760–1826): SuperStock Ltd.
Page 74: Water rushing over Rocks: The Image Bank.
Page 77: *Crucifixion*, by Diego Rodriguez de Silva y Velázquez (1599–1660): Prado, Madrid/Bridgeman Art Library, London/New York.
Page 80: Signpost: Nicholas Rous.
Page 84: Sun: SuperStock Ltd.

Page 88: *Lament of Christ by the Virgin and St John*, 1614/15 (panel), by Peter Paul Rubens (1577–1640): Künsthistorisches Museum, Vienna/Bridgeman Art Library, London/New York.
Page 91: *The Delivery of Israel out of Egypt* (oil on canvas), by Samuel Colman (1780–1845): Birmingham Museums and Art Gallery/Bridgeman Art Library, London/New York.
Page 94–95: Pathway: The Image Bank.
Page 100: Cave: Tony Stone Images.
Page 103: *Triptych of the Day*, by Gaetano Previati (1852–1920): SuperStock Ltd.
Page 105: *Noli me Tangere*, after Mantegna: copyright © The National Gallery, London.
Page 109: *The Procession to Calvary*, by Ridolfo Ghirlandaio (1483–1561): copyright © The National Gallery, London.
Page 110: Rock: Tony Stone Images.
Page 113: Marvao, Portugal: Superstock Ltd.
Page 118: *Christ served by Angels*, 1650 (fresco), by Baldassare Franceschini (Il Volterrano) (1611–89): Museo della Pittura Murale, Prato/Bridgeman Art Library, London/New York.
Page 123: Pathway: Telegraph Colour Library.